WESTERN WRITERS SERIES

No. 40

C. L. SONNICHSEN

by Joyce Gibson Roach

BOISE STATE UNIVERSITY
BOISE, IDAHO

Boise State University Western Writers Series   Number 40

C. L. Sonnichsen

By Joyce Gibson Roach

Editors: Wayne Chatterton
James H. Maguire

Business Manager:
James Hadden

Cover Design and Illustration
by Arny Skov, Copyright 1979

Boise State University, Boise, Idaho

Copyright 1979
by the
Boise State University Western Writers Series

ALL RIGHTS RESERVED

Library of Congress Card No. 79-53653

International Standard Book No. 0-88430-064-1

Printed in the United States of America by
The Caxton Printers, Ltd.
Caldwell, Idaho

C.L. Sonnichsen

C. L. Sonnichsen

El Paso is located at almost the farthest point of West Texas, where the Rio Grande River begins its sweep into the Big Bend country. Strangers find it a region extreme in its limitless supply of nothing. Even natives joke about the area. It is a place where "every living thing seems prepared to fight for its life. Even the plants go armed and hardly a shrub can be found without a spine or fang somewhere" (*Roy Bean,* p. 71). Texans do not expect a man from Minnesota with a Ph.D. from Harvard to write affectionately about the sand, sun, and stickers; to embrace that region's history as his own; or to find anything amusing about the climate.

Charles Leland Sonnichsen did. For over forty years he has been writing about the country around El Paso encompassing Arizona and New Mexico and portions of Old Mexico. He is something of a folklorist and an excellent historian and humorist. But none of these separate labels fits exactly. By his own definition, C. L. Sonnichsen is a "grassroots historian," one who works "in out-of-the-way places, reads country newspapers, prowls about the county courthouses, and spends a lot of time interviewing old men and women" ("Grassroots Historian," *Southwest Historical Quarterly,* p. 381).

He also ranges the borderlands that connect history, literature, and sociology. One of his specialties is frontier violence. He knows a great deal about cattlemen, gamblers, and a myriad of other frontier folk and how they came to be. His current interest lies in history and folklore as they appear in Southwestern and Western fiction. If he has to have a label, then, Sonnichsen might also be labeled a folk historian.

C. L. Sonnichsen was born September 20, 1901, in Iowa. He came from what we are fond of classifying as typically American stock — hard working farm people who moved around the newly settled frontier trying to find land and better times. Sonnichsen's father, Henry, suffered from both asthma and poverty. He decided to turn away from the damp Iowa climate and to look somewhere else to remedy both conditions. Minnesota held promise, and Henry, his wife Mary, and the baby, Charles Leland, moved to a place near Hancock.

The family moved with a trainload of other homeseekers. The trip proved a traumatic experience, especially for the Sonnichsen livestock. With the family possessions reduced to the smallest size, Henry padded the roof of the boxcar to prevent the livestock from beating their brains out. Sonnichsen remembers, however, that "one cow lost her mind during the trip and never did get it back" (*A Memoir of Henry and Mary Sonnichsen*, p. 46). The family stayed near Hancock and bore two more sons — Lloyd, who died in 1917, and Harold, who later became a prominent chemist. In 1916 the family moved to Wadena, where Sonnichsen attended high school and graduated third in his class.

Sonnichsen remembers that his father liked to work "and worked as hard as he could, with something like joy, all his life" (*Memoir*, p. 76). The family schedule consisted of getting up early, doing hard work, going to bed a little after dark, reading the Bible, and getting ready for church on Saturday. Mary Sonnichsen worked equally hard but made time for other pursuits outside the farm. She was a Seventh-Day Adventist, a staunch member of the Women's Christian Temperance Union, a prohibitionist, a Bible reader and hymn singer — altogether a strong-minded woman. All in all, this life was a good upbringing for a boy who would have to make his way alone and without financial help until he had obtained a Ph.D. degree.

In 1920 Sonnichsen enrolled at the University of Minnesota. This venture was an enormous undertaking for a farm boy with no money. A letter from Sonnichsen's brother Harold reveals much of what college meant to the family at a time when things became steadily worse economically. Their situation was depressing, but Harold remembered that one of the good things about their life was his mother's and father's pride in their first son's experience at college. Each week, Leland faithfully and cheerfully wrote of his progress. Harold recalled, "Leland's letters were always read aloud as soon as the three of us could be together. . . . Mother tore them open eagerly and read them as soon as they came and then usually reread them to us, savoring the good news and laughing at the jokes. It was a good deal more than hearing news from a well-loved son — it was a window on a larger and better world which they must sometimes have doubted could exist. Their days were filled with so much physical effort and worry over small emergencies that it was a tonic to them to know that there were such things as college glee clubs and courses in dead languages" (*Memoir,* p. 72).

In addition to the simpler pleasures, there were serious ones too. English literature and creative writing were Sonnichsen's major subjects, and Italian was his minor. He graduated *cum laude*. Though he had hoped to add *magna* to the title, he unfortunately gave an unpopular answer to the question: What is the most important quality in literature? His answer was that he thought it ought to be interesting (Interview, May 1971).

After receiving his B.A. degree at the University of Minnesota in 1924, Sonnichsen served as assistant master at St. James military high school in Minnesota. He remembers with a laugh that most of the residents had problems of one kind or another and that his chief contribution there was that he had served as supervisor of the Bed Wetting Squad (Interview, May 1971).

Sonnichsen took his M.A. degree in 1927 and his Ph.D. in 1931 at Harvard, where his specialty was English literature of the seventeenth and eighteenth centuries. His dissertation on Thomas Sprat, Bishop of Rochester, won for him the Bowdoin Prize at Harvard in 1931. Research also taught him that not all valuable information is in books. Sonnichsen completed much of his research by corresponding with informants in England, and he was able to gather a valuable collection of Sprat's writings and sermons for the Harvard library.

Sonnichsen encountered famous men at Harvard, Chester Noyes Greenough, George Lyman Kittredge, and Irving Babbitt among them. Sonnichsen remembers a remark which Babbitt made when that scholar was asked whether he thought the young men of his day were immoral. "No," he replied. "They are not immoral. They are merely unbuttoned" (Interview, May 1971).

Sonnichsen says that he came to Texas in 1931 by way of the Harvard Glee Club. Because he was away from the campus on tour with the club, he missed most of the job interviews. After employment at Carnegie Tech for two years — 1927 to 1929 — he applied at what was then the Texas College of Mines in El Paso. He probably got the job because he had had experience teaching at a technological school, and that teaching experience was a result of his missing other job interviews. This chain of events brings us back to the Harvard Glee Club.

A dissertation on Bishop Sprat and tours with the Harvard Glee Club had hardly prepared Sonnichsen for what he was about to encounter at the Texas College of Mines. Before coming he had found out that teaching American Literature, about which he knew very little, would be one of his assignments. But there was worse to come. John B. Barry, the school's first president, informed Sonnichsen that he would also be teaching a course entitled "Life and Literature of the Southwest." The new teacher doubted that there was any such literature, but even if there were, he was not inclined to learn about it. Yet Sonnichsen taught the course and was thereby initiated into things Southwestern.

Before coming to Texas, Sonnichsen had been deeply involved in interesting and demanding research. He wished for some new scholarly commitment and seriously thought of Samuel Butler's *Hudibras* as a topic for study. He intended to remain an eighteenth-century man, but circumstances changed his mind. For one thing, the library was contained not in a building, but in one room on the campus, and it was noticeably short on *Hudibras* material. The research would have to be done in England, not in the Texas desert, and there was no way to get to England. President Dossie M. Wiggins's attitude toward research and publication was another factor. At a faculty meeting Wiggins informed his teachers that they were hired to teach and that if they wanted to do research it would be done on their own. "I hire faculty members," he added, "as if I were buying mules. I try to get as much as I can for my money" ("Harvard on the Border," *Nova,* June 1974, p. 13).

Though still contemplating further research in Butler, Sonnichsen pondered the strange landscape and border environment where he now found himself, and decided to attend a meeting of the Texas Folklore Society. Here a southwestward course was again steered for him. He was elected president. The members who conducted, and still conduct, their business with a loose rein, wanted to hold a joint meeting with the New Mexico Folklore Society. El Paso was a convenient location, and an El Paso man was needed to make the arrangements. The first man from El Paso to show up at a meeting was going to be elected president whether he liked it or not.

After that, Sonnichsen ceased to look across the sea for his area of study. He developed instead an absorbing interest in the history, folklore, landscape, and fiction of the Southwest and became, as J. Frank Dobie once phrased it about another Westerner, "a man suitable to his time and place" ("Harvard on the Border," p. 11). Sonnichsen soon discovered that the feuding, fussing, and fighting Texans were worthy successors to the bear baiters in *Hudibras* and that the best approach to his Southwestern subjects was through a combination of research in courthouse records, newspapers, books, and archives and of interviewing people who could still remember the way things had been.

If Sonnichsen ever looked wistfully back to the Eastern strongholds of scholarship, no one ever knew. He set about making the desert country his own, learning to speak proficient Spanish, assimilating border culture and lore so that he soon surpassed the natives in knowledge of the region, and tackling with enthusiasm the problems of teaching at a border university. Sonnichsen taught for forty-one years in El Paso and was without a doubt one of the most popular teachers on the campus. He became head of the English department in 1933, was Graduate Dean from 1960 to 1967, and was named Harry Yandell Benedict Professor in 1966 and Piper Professor in 1971. His course in Southwest Literature became something of a legend where a student might learn border ballads, or be introduced to all kinds of border folk, or expand his knowledge of the region during his lifetime by referring to Sonnichsen's mimeographed bibliography of "The Southwest: The Record in Books," which kept growing each year and which Sonnichsen always gave to his students. After his retirement from the University in 1971, Sonnichsen moved to Tucson, Arizona, where he served as senior editor of the *Journal of Arizona History* until 1978.

Sonnichsen's books fall generally into three categories of

subject matter: (1) frontier folk, (2) feuding, and (3) history. His published works will here be treated according to these categories.

Newcomers to the Southwest are often drawn to the unusual people who have lived there. *Billy King's Tombstone: The Private Life of an Arizona Boom Town* was written in 1935 but not published until 1943. Sonnichsen here takes on, in his first book, the people and the town which is among the most fabulous of all frontier settlements.

Billy King was a cowboy, gambler, saloon keeper, and peace officer. He pursued these varied careers from 1882 to 1905 during the best years — or worst, depending upon one's point of view — of the town's existence. Billy's story was brought to Sonnichsen's attention by Mrs. Charles Heid of El Paso, who knew and looked after the old man. When the two met, Billy agreed to tell Sonnichsen all he remembered.

Writing about Tombstone or the people who lived there was not a new idea. Walter Noble Burns' *Tombstone* (1927) and Stuart Lake's *Wyatt Earp: Frontier Marshal* (1931) had already set the public's mind ablaze with the "truth" about the town and its famous citizens. Both books passed as factual accounts even though the Tombstone that they depicted was peopled with figures whose behavior smacked of characters from Arthurian legend, while their Wyatt Earp had the stance of a Gary Cooper ("Tombstone in Fiction," *Journal of Arizona History*, Vol. 19, Summer 1968, p. 59). When Sonnichsen began writing *Billy King's Tombstone* in 1935, there were already factual and fictional books about that wide place in the road. All purported to be the truth and all added to the rosy haze that hung over the town. Sonnichsen was one of the first to penetrate the fog, and if he found men who were less than heroes, he discovered some human beings whose behavior was, to use Dobie's phrase again, suitable to their time and place.

This theme of suitability to time and place runs through many of Sonnichsen's books and provides his explanation of the frontier code. Sonnichsen does not deny that our own frontier period was our heroic age and that the inhabitants of Tombstone are worthy of heroic labels. At the same time, he is not ashamed to point out that most of the heroes came from the wrong part of town.

As in most small towns, the sides of the street are symbolic. In Tombstone the proper folks went about their business on the south side of town, whereas the gamblers, saloon keepers, gunslingers, and prostitutes lived on the north side. And it is the north side that Sonnichsen writes about. If the reader is looking for the Earps and Clantons in the O.K. Corral, he will have to look in someone else's book. Sonnichsen's story, set in a time just after the Earps, gives us glimpses of Rotten Row with its frontier lawyers; of Buckskin Frank Leslie, whose dress in keeping with his nickname, helped in the creation of his dramatic figure; of gamblers and high rollers such as Sleepy Tom Thomas; of Dick Clark, who taught Billy King something about cards; and of Fatty Ryan, as well as Pete Spence, who went in for stage robbery to supplement their incomes. Also living on the north side were the Boom Town Belles. There were brave men and good in Tombstone, men such as John Slaughter the lawman and Doc Goodfellow, who ministered to Mexican, Indian, and White, to rich and poor.

Sonnichsen calls our attention to the unheroic with a humorous approach. He feels no need to rub our noses in the facts. Making witty comments about situations which some would consider frightening, bewildering, or even bad is typical of C. L. Sonnichsen. The pleasantly sharp point of his humor is appropriate to his subjects in the Southwest where the landscape is often barbed, the people tough, and the situation thorny. In speaking of Buckskin Leslie's career at its height, for example, Sonnichsen writes: "At that moment he wouldn't have known how to ask for any more than life offered him. People whispered behind his back. . . . He was discussed in every bar and poolroom in the West from Fort Worth to Sacramento" (*Billy King's Tombstone,* p. 32).

As stated above, *Billy King's Tombstone* was written in 1935 but not published until 1943. It took the eight years to find a publisher, Sonnichsen believes, because in the thirties "the demand was still for journalistic history or Zane Grey-type fiction" (*Billy King's Tombstone,* preface). Upon publication, the book was favorably reviewed in the New York *Herald Tribune* of July 19, 1943, and the New York *Times* of May 23, 1943. In looking back Sonnichsen wonders whether, as he puts it, it was not a little "smart-alecky" in style (Interview, Tucson, August 1974). If so, it did nothing to hurt the book, which after all was filled with many smart-alecky people. Both the characters and Sonnichsen have a good time, and so does the reader.

Telling of the array of wildly versatile townspeople in Tombstone was a good warming-up exercise for Sonnichsen in this first book. He takes obvious pleasure in the panorama of the streets of Tombstone, and he has a verbal romp with the people he finds there. They are good fun, and the author might have built a solid writing reputation on just such humorous circumstances. Sonnichsen, however, knew that certain frontiersmen such as Roy Bean were more important than others to an understanding of the region. Since he did not grow up with the Roy Bean story, Sonnichsen was not misled by thinking he knew all about it. He treated Roy Bean material as if it were all brand new and tried to separate the actualities from the lore. Sonnichsen collected facts about Bean, and that gave him something definitive to say about folk heroes in general. His research for *Roy Bean* continued over four years before publication of the book in 1943. His purpose was to "look into his history and see how a Roy Bean ever came to be at all" (*Roy Bean*, p. 54).

While popular interest has focused on Bean's career as a justice of the peace who practiced flamboyantly in Langtry, Texas, Sonnichsen traces Bean's wanderings before his late entrance into the law. Sonnichsen makes use of books, old newspapers, court records, and people who knew and remembered Bean. There are stories of Roy's pet bear and of his platonic, long-distanced relationship with Lily Langtry, whom he never met but after whom he named his town. We learn of Bean's quarrels with his wife. His somewhat odd personal appearance is related to an incident in his early years when he barely escaped hanging and was left with a stiff neck. As a result Bean had to turn his whole body in order to see. Well known stories are told and some that are not so well known. Sonnichsen tells about the time when Roy was running a dairy. There were so many customers that Roy began watering down the milk to make it go further. A local judge knew what was going on and told Bean that he would like his milk and water in separate buckets, for he had found a minnow in his milk. Roy rose to the occasion by responding "By God! . . . that's what comes of watering them cows at the river!" (*Roy Bean*, p. 59).

Sonnichsen uses Roy Bean to illustrate certain features of all heroes. First, the hero must be fairly ignorant, making him one of the crowd. Too much book learning is viewed with suspicion, as being inconsistent with horse sense. The really wise man is a "natural" man, knowing only what he reads in the papers. Smartness, not to be confused with education, is necessary for outwitting lesser men. Poverty is helpful. The hero must be either brave or a good bluffer. Most important of all, the hero must do everything — even his lying — on a grand scale. If the facts of a prospective idol's life do not measure up, legend will supply the details. Sonnichsen adds another dimension to the study of the folk hero: sometimes the hero himself is aware of his role and often helps the legend along in his own lifetime by dressing and acting the part.

Roy Bean believed in himself as a folk hero, and he did what he could to further the myth. He wanted the spotlight, always preferring "to strut in a yard just big enough for himself" (*Roy Bean,* p. 54). Roy used many weapons — ranting, swearing, strutting, and humor. If Roy Bean was set on making himself a frontier hero, then Sonnichsen is set on making us look at what Bean really was and causing us to like what we see. When all the façade is stripped away, there is simply a dirty old man, unredeemable; but when the facts are bedizened with the humor of Bean himself and with that of Sonnichsen's treatment of him, Roy is bearable, even likeable. One example of Sonnichsen's humor concerns the ways some West Texans met their death:

> People died for strange reasons in those days. Some got up too early to see well and threw a saddle on somebody else's horse. Others got stray calves tangled up in their loops. Many a man died on account of clerical errors made with a branding iron, and many more passed on because of misplaced confidence in a poker hand or a tendency to dilly-dally in drawing their six shooters. . . . Strangely enough one of the favorite ways of leaving the world in West Texas at that time was falling off a bridge. This was partly because there were so many opportunities and partly because there were so many accidents. The railroad had to build bridges over dozens of arroyos and canyons . . . and most of them were suitable places for a mishap. The high bridge over the Pecos, however, was the most dangerous. It was over three hundred feet above the floor of the canyon and was the natural

selection of anyone looking for a bridge to fall off of. (*Roy Bean*, p. 124)

Many reviewers praised *Roy Bean*, among them Joseph Jackson of the San Francisco *Chronicle*. He wrote: "Mr. Sonnichsen is that rare creature, a student of folk-history and a good writer to boot" (March 4, 1943). Even now the public still likes the book. It has been reissued twice, once in paperback. Other writers have, of course, noticed Roy Bean. Some had written books about him before Sonnichsen. Everett Lloyd's *Law West of the Pecos* and Ruel McDaniel's *Vinegaroon* are two. Both are filled with Bean anecdotes, but both authors were newspapermen and made no attempt to do more than repeat yarns. Sonnichsen's book was the first and only one to try to establish the facts about Bean and to authenticate the stories. Sonnichsen actually found people who were there when some of the events happened, and he was even able to interview people who knew Bean or his family. As Sonnichsen remembers, "I came along at just the right time and very shortly after I did my gathering, it was too late to do any more" (Letter, September 10, 1975).

In *Cowboys and Cattle Kings*, published in 1950, Sonnichsen returns to a group of people. The book is actually a report sponsored by the Rockefeller Committee at the University of Oklahoma, and it is about the modern-day inheritors of the frontier cattle industry. Sonnichsen visited the small enterprises, feedlots, old style ranches, and even the dude ranches to determine how the modern cattlemen are faring and what changes have taken place in the business.

Sonnichsen found all the old problems in abundance. The weather in all its extremes is still a menace, but at the end of his era the old-time rancher ran up against a problem — the encroachment of civilization — which has been replaced by a real monster — the helpful hand of the government. Becoming involved of necessity with lobbyists, lawyers, and national organizations, cattlemen have often become their own worst press agents. Most ranchers in talking about the government fall back on the tenets of their unwritten code: a cattleman takes care of himself; let every other man do likewise.

Sonnichsen's conclusion is that in the modern cattle business, it takes all kinds of cattlemen from feedlot operators to weekend ranchers. Generally, however, they all possess qualities which make them kin to their predecessors — independent spirits, tenacious dispositions, hospitable natures, and the hopeful outlook that "if the Lord is willin' and the creek don't rise," everything will be all right.

The sources for Sonnichsen's study were mostly oral. Rather than relating mere facts, he tells stories about the people he met, allowing the reader to observe the cattle industry from the point of view of the people in it. If the book is a report, Sonnichsen wisely lets the people do their own reporting. From the Klebergs of the fabled King Ranch to the old stove-up cowboy who laments that his Levis don't hold up as well as they did forty years ago, the book is a gem of a collection about cow ways and cow folks. Whatever statistics and changes the author records, they are never so important as his human beings.

J. Frank Dobie did not like *Cowboys and Cattle Kings,* but Walter Prescott Webb, Dobie's colleague on the faculty of the University of Texas, did. In the January 1951 issue of the *American Historical Journal,* Webb gave this tribute: "He has brought something new in subject matter to the history of the cattle kingdom, and it is unique, without a competitor. . . . Since it is a primary source, there is little for the critic to find fault with. If the author made errors which so delight the critic, they are a secret between him and Brand Inspector Chase Feagins of Alliance, Nebraska, or Mrs. Laura-He-Does-It of Crow Agency, Montana, . . . or hundreds of others interviewed from the Rio Grande to the Canadian border. . . . In short, the whole book is out of the old cattle kingdom where men still live who know whether a book about them and their cows is any good" (pp. 365-66).

New York paid some attention to the book. Stanley Walker wrote: "An ambitious project and never before attempted in quite this detailed-over-all fashion. He brings in just enough about the old timers, and the history of the business, to put the present day cattle raiser in proper focus" (New York *Herald Tribune,* October 15, 1950).

In *Alias Billy the Kid,* written in collaboration with William Morrison in 1955, Sonnichsen turns again to a particular person, a man who claimed to have been The Kid, but who went by the name of Brushy Bill Roberts. Brushy Bill was one of those characters you hear of now and then and one that no writer could possibly leave alone. Brushy Bill came to Sonnichsen's attention when Morrison, a lawyer, brought him the story of a man who claimed to be the Billy the Kid shot by Pat Garrett in Pete Maxwell's yard in July 1881.

In 1948, Morrison, an expert in historical research, was serving as attorney for a man who claimed to be a survivor of the Lincoln County War. The client told Morrison that his friend, Billy the Kid, was still living too. Morrison found the resurrected ninety-year-old Kid in Hico, Texas, in 1949. He interviewed him, documented some of the old man's statements, believed him, and then arranged for an interview with Governor Mabry of New Mexico. The governor, historians, and relatives of people involved in stories of Billy cross-examined the man, frightened him badly, and then determined that he was not genuine. Morrison, however, believed in the man — Ollie L. Roberts, alias Brushy Bill, alias Rattlesnake Bill, alias Texas Kid, alias Hugo Kid, alias Billy the Kid, alias William Bonney, alias William Antrim — and took his evidence to Sonnichsen.

It was too strange and fascinating a story to keep out of print, and the resulting book offers new stories, new facts, new interpretations, and new contradictions. The authors knew that skeptics would not believe their story, but they point out in the prologue that a lawyer and a college professor, more than ordinarily respectful of "sources, verification and evidence," would not deliberately attempt to deceive. They propose to let Billy tell his own story, while they offer newspaper accounts, correspondence, corroborating testimony, and official records in support of his claim.

Before incredulous readers can raise a host of questions, the authors are already two jumps ahead. They point out that Brushy Bill was too illiterate to have read up on the subject, that he was too well informed to have been an outsider, that oral sources could not have provided the detailed accounts he gave, and that only someone who had been there at the precise time of the happenings could have told such a story. Nonbelievers are faced with the question, "if Brushy Bill Roberts wasn't Billy the Kid, then who was he?" (*Billy the Kid,* p. 98).

Alias Billy the Kid is more limited in scope than most of Sonnichsen's books. The authors are careful to note that Sonnichsen's other regional heroes, heroines, outlaws, and feuders have meaning in broader areas of lore; but Bill's story is offered without attaching deeper meanings. It is still a good and curious story. Stanley Vestal agreed: "Bushy Bill's story is well worth a reader's time, and a notable addition to the legend of Billy the Kid. If you are familiar with the legend, this book will give you something to think about and argue over" (*Oklahoman,* July 17, 1955).

Brushy Bill needed little help in telling his story, but Bill Mitchell was an outlaw who was fortunate to have had such a writer as C. L. Sonnichsen explain the events of his life. In many ways, *Outlaw: Bill Mitchell Alias Baldy Russell, His Life and Times* (1965) is one of the author's best books because of its portrayal of outlaws. Sonnichsen refers to this favorite among his books as his "step-child" because it was not given much notice by the critics. He felt that his special contribution was in "taking on an outlaw and showing how it was for him from beginning to end" (Interview, August 7, 1971).

Outlaw is not just another story about a typical bad man. The general reading public makes heroes of some outlaws, believing that there are "Good Bad Men and Bad Bad Men" (*Outlaw,* p. 15). The author wished to show in his story of one outlaw the things that are generally overlooked, such as the different motives involved when people choose sides and fight, the hardships suffered by the outlaw's family, the juxtaposition in attitudes of hatred and kindness, the generosity and vengefulness present in the same person, and the erosive power of an inhospitable environment.

Bill Mitchell's trouble was family trouble. Bill's father was unjustly hanged for his part in a feud with the Truitt family over a piece of land on the Brazos River near Granbury, Texas. Bill was an "unlettered, violent, bitter man with an ingrained and inbred belief that he must resist and revenge all personal affronts" (*Outlaw,* p. 58). He avenged the death of his father by walking quietly into the home of James Truitt and shooting him in the head. For the next forty-seven years Bill Mitchell assumed the name of Baldy Russell and lived in the wilds of New Mexico. How the family lived, that is, existed, in a dugout brings into focus how Bill's family also had to pay for his crime. His little girls' longing to read and wanting to play a violin which Bill has bought; his wife's spending much of her time scanning the horizon; the coincidental wandering of some Truitt relatives into Bill's camp — all these make for poignant drama.

Bill Mitchell and his family lived forty-seven years outside the law in hardship and pain because of a few minutes of revenge. But, as Sonnichsen points out, Bill's story "explains a little of what we ought to understand about the kind of people who settled the West, the kind of rules they lived by, the terrible deeds they could do when they felt called upon, the punishments they were willing to endure for the sake of their special codes" (*Outlaw,* p. 25).

Critics ignored *Outlaw,* possibly because Bill Mitchell did not behave like Billy the Kid or Jesse James. Publishers were not interested for the same reason. Bill was something of an original, as perhaps were all outlaws until folklore translated them into something tastier. Mitchell fulfilled all the requirements of a bad-man hero; but nobody ever knew or cared, for he ran away into the desert. That a bad-man hero must never do if he would be reckoned a hero. To be a hero, however, was never Bill's ambition. While he interested neither his neighbors nor the critics, his life makes extremely fascinating reading.

From the beginning, Sonnichsen was able to write about frontier folk from the point of view of their suitability to their time and place. Viewed on a world scale, some of them did not amount to much, but if a reader could look at them, as Sonnichsen has him look at Roy Bean, from the perspective of how they fitted into their own environment, most of these characters are worthy of notice. Some such as Colonel William Cornell Greene stood considerably above the crowd and attracted national notice. In *Colonel Greene and the Copper Skyrocket,* published by the University of Arizona Press in 1974, Sonnichsen tells about a man who, along with others, owed his fortune to Thomas A. Edison. The invention of the electric light with its power lines of copper made that mineral in demand. Colonel Greene's story concerns more than copper. His interests reached beyond mining and into ranching. He crossed the paths of Apaches, bandits, investors to whom he tried to sell stock, and even the governments of Arizona, New York, and Mexico.

Sonnichsen had much help from Greene's family in writing the book. Naturally they wanted a sympathetic portrayal of the man who had had bad things said about him during his lifetime and after. It is to the author's credit that he was able to defend Greene and at the same time show his weaknesses only as signs of his humanity. Ben Capps feels that Sonnichsen "manages to show a vigorous, brilliant gambling entrepreneur with faults as well as virtues." Capps also notes that the author "is not above fictionalizing as when he opens a chapter with imaginary dialogue between two characters" (Ft. Worth *Star Telegram*, June 13, 1974). Harwood Hinton emphasizes that "at times the book reads like a novel, for Sonnichsen's prose is lively and vivid" (El Paso *Times*, July 13, 1974). Sonnichsen was awarded the Western Heritage Award from the Cowboy Hall of Fame for this biography.

The personal codes of the frontiersmen are always given sympathetic treatment by Sonnichsen. He is definitely a "code of the West" man. Neither condoning nor condemning, he tries to understand when he can the behavior of people who were very often either glamorized or condemned or laughed off as merely colorful. His explanation of their codes helps the reader to see them as they were — like us, human beings capable of terrible sins and monumental goodness.

Many of Sonnichsen's stories about frontier people involve their personal quarrels with others. When a group of people take violent issue with another group, that violence is called a feud. Texas has had its share of such conflicts, and C. L. Sonnichsen has sought the people, causes, and results of some of the livelier vendettas.

Soon after becoming a Texan, Sonnichsen became acquainted with the opprobrious custom of feuding. After investigating the dispute at Richmond, Texas, known as the Jaybird-Woodpecker feud, Sonnichsen began to keep files on other Texas vendettas. The results of his research were *I'll Die Before I'll Run* (1951), *Ten Texas Feuds* (1957), *Tularosa: Last of the Frontier West* (1960), and *The El Paso Salt War* (1961).

The reconstruction of feuds could prove an insurmountable task. Writing about them, especially when the participants or descendants are close enough to lay hands on the author, could prove dangerous. Sonnichsen thinks the physical danger is minimal, but he admits that his feud material was difficult to handle. At first, from 1935 to 1955, the difficulty came not from informants but from prospective publishers. The Dallas *News* considered it bad policy to stir up unpleasant memories for descendants of a South Texas dispute. New York publishers wanted action pictures such as corpses in morgues and hanging bodies, in spite of the fact that photographers were rarely conspicuous guests during or after illegal lynchings. Regionally, during those years, there was a strong feeling against published accounts of violence. Sonnichsen points out that the aversion to violence was justified, because the sensational and notorious actions of frontiersmen have often resulted in untruthful, romanticized accounts. The grassroots historian, no matter how serious his investigation, was looked upon with suspicion ("Grassroots Historian," p. 384).

Sonnichsen found that it was not easy to question people about family scandals. One lady he was interviewing cried, and some asked him not to publish things that would bring the family shame. He honored those requests, and consequently there are still some stories waiting to be told when there is no survivor to weep over the family honor. Most people, however, he found helpful so long as he approached in an open, friendly way: "I knew . . . that if I talked straight and kept my hands in sight, I would probably survive — and I have" ("Grassroots Historian," p. 391).

Sonnichsen's first feud book, *I'll Die Before I'll Run,* is important in its portrayal of the philosophy of feuding. The book details the particulars of the Jaybird-Woodpecker feud in Richmond, Texas, in 1889, the feud which first prompted Sonnichsen to look into the subject. Sonnichsen points out that there seemed to have been different types of feuds, depending on the era in which they occurred. Feuds in the 1860's were often based on Civil War troubles. Feuds in the 1870's saw the heyday of the outlaw and the hired gun. The 1880's brought barbed wire and a confrontation of sheepmen and cattlemen, while feuding in the 1890's was usually over family troubles.

His study of feuding has brought Sonnichsen to the conclusion that Texas feuders all fought their battles differently. He describes feuding in such places as the Kentucky mountains and offers comparisons with Texas troubles. He notes that mountain feuds are thought of as family affairs, as being caused by something trivial, and as taking place among illiterate people in isolated places. The motivation of Texas feuds does not necessarily follow that pattern, but they may begin when individuals or groups decide that they have been grievously wronged, their code violated. They take the law, which has not protected them, into their own hands. This kind of action, unlawful as it may appear, helps assist the law even if it resorts to unlawful means to do it. It should be noted as well that feuds often occur not only among the rebellious, but also among the conservative elements of society.

Sonnichsen explains that feuding seems more prevalent in the South because of ancestral custom. He traces the tradition of personal family honor to the English, who settled the South. In Texas, the Southern tradition became mixed with the idea of frontier justice and self-redress. The Texas code figures in a bit of folklore which declares that you can tell the place from which a man comes by the way he behaves when you call him a liar. A Texan shoots you or knocks you down. A man from Ohio shakes his fist and shouts, "You're another." The New Englander "spits on a grasshopper and remarks calmly, 'Well you can't prove it'" (*I'll Die Before I'll Run,* p. 9).

Do feuds follow a pattern? Sonnichsen believes they do. The feud usually begins over some intolerable conditions or over a violation of a person's sense of right. Another part of the pattern is that the persons involved must decide to fight or run. If they decide to fight, people — good Christian people — grow accustomed to the idea of killing and lose their scruples about how it is done. Seldom does the fighting die out of its own accord; instead, it gets worse and worse.

Before Harper and Brothers accepted *I'll Die Before I'll Run,* the publisher insisted that Sonnichsen cut some of his material. There were enough stories left to make another feud book. *Ten Texas Feuds* demonstrates further that Texans had a predilection for fighting, had many tools to do it with, and had more than enough opportunities for practice. The book was widely and favorably reviewed in publications from the New York *Times* to the *Sheep and Goat Raiser* to the *Brand Book of English Westerners*. Ray Colwell in the *Denver Westerners* (September 1958) enthusiastically commented that "no one in his right mind is going to take exception to either the literary or historical quality of anything that comes from the pen of Dr. Sonnichsen . . . ." Frederick W. Nolan of England declared that it was "wonderfully good reading" (*Brand Book of English Westerners*, mimeographed review, 1958). A New York reviewer was less impressed, saying that "sometimes it is difficult to tell who is shooting at whom and why. Nevertheless these are minor shortcomings . . ." (New York *Times,* January 1, 1958). Sonnichsen was honored for *Ten Texas Feuds* by being named one of the top Texas writers at the Annual Writers Round-Up in Austin in 1958.

Tularosa: *Last of the Frontier West* may have been intended as another feud book, but it is also an excellent commentary upon frontier cattlemen and the standards which set them apart from other men on the frontier. It is one of Sonnichsen's most popular books, and it won for him the Theta Sigma Phi Annual Writers Round-Up Award in 1960.

Some researchers have developed a romantic thesis about cow people which asserts that they were noble and pure knights of chivalrous proportions engaged in but a new kind of tournament. Other writers view cattlemen as the antithesis of all that is honorable and good, as destroyers bent on making profit at the expense of others. Sonnichsen's opinion represents the synthesis of other viewpoints by showing that the cattleman was both good and bad, chivalrous and ignoble, and that it is unfair to judge him by the standards of another time or place. He lived in a place that had been, for the most part, uninhabitable, and by his own methods and standards, he brought the land into usefulness. *Tularosa* is really all about those standards which came to be known as the code of the cattleman and about the men who lived by that code. Feuding is often a natural consequence of the enactment of the code, and in that sense the book is another study of feuding, particularly the feud between A. J. Fountain and Oliver Lee.

The area that Fountain and Lee called home is an arid locale some thirty miles wide and two hundred miles long, stretching north of El Paso, Texas, and Alamogordo, New Mexico. While it is true that Texans introduced cattle to the area, Sonnichsen says that the "cow would have voted against the step if she had been asked" (*Tularosa,* p. 3).

Before describing the cattlemen's troubles, which he learned about from published and from firsthand sources, Sonnichsen explains the set of rules by which the cattlemen were playing an often deadly game. The first essential in the cowman's unwritten constitution was courage. Running from a fight or quitting before a conclusion was reached showed cowardice.

Loyalty amounting to clannishness, the next prerequisite, bound him to friends whether they were right or wrong, whether they won or lost. A man was expected to finish any job he started, to be tolerant of the weak, never to inquire about another's past, to be cheerful under grueling assignments, and to ask no man to right another man's wrongs. These fundamental qualities, along with the habit of carrying side arms, often culminated in the most salient feature of the code — murder. According to the creed, it was right to kill a man to avenge a personal insult, to punish him for robbery, or simply to eliminate him because he "needed killing." It is well to remember that both the "good guys" and the "bad guys" played by these same rules, and that is why it becomes difficult to tell the heroes from the villains.

In addition to Fountain and Lee's troubles we meet interesting people in *Tularosa* — such people as Eugene Manlove Rhodes. Sonnichsen's main concern is with Rhodes's life as a cattleman rather than with his career as a writer. Gene Rhodes was a close friend of Oliver Lee and a cattleman of the same brand. Certainly Rhodes's upbringing in the traditions of the cowman's code influenced his writing. Sonnichsen finds that Rhodes's dialogue, which features plenty of homespun humor, was characteristic of real cowmen in spite of the fact that other writers of Rhodes's day stereotyped them as strong, silent humorless types. Many local characters and incidents of New Mexico life appear in Rhodes's stories, and yet Sonnichsen found no mention of the Fountain-Lee affair. He suggests that Rhodes could not believe such a thing, especially about his friends. Rhodes apparently believed in his own Western myth.

Sonnichsen ends the chapter with a portion of Rhodes's memorable "Hired Man on Horseback." It is a fitting conclusion to the story of frontier cattlemen whom Sonnichsen has so expertly and sympathetically treated. One could wish he had ended the book there, but he adds other chapters on Pat Garrett, on the Three Rivers area, and on how space enterprises are sending frontiersmen to other frontiers. The chapters are somewhat anticlimactic but perhaps helpful in showing a convincing picture of the destiny of the Tularosa area.

Sonnichsen's method in Tularosa is effective in showing how complex feuds may be. When the reader has had enough facts and names and insinuations about whose cows are in what pens, the author stops. Interspersed among these chapters on the continuing troubles between cattlemen, are chapters on such subjects as the railroad, a French recluse, Albert Fall, and A. J. Fountain. Breaking into the main action with those chapters on other subjects makes the book more interesting.

Tularosa is one of Sonnichsen's most readable books, possibly because the disputes are subservient to the strong personalities of the characters. The book was popular and received good reviews. The Houston *Chronicle* noted Sonnichsen's method and commented that he "has a knack of unearthing little known but significant facts and of relating them in an informal, sometimes disjointed, but always highly interesting style" (August 4, 1960). Lon Tinkle said: "Sonnichsen . . . long has made the unwritten history of the Old West his special domain. This is the eighth of his books to demonstrate that he has a sixth sense for getting close-mouthed old-timers and their descendants to talk straight and to lend letters and documentation. Once he has gathered the details, he writes them up with impressive skill" (Chicago *Tribune,* August 6, 1960). The Los Angeles *Times* sums up Sonnichsen's approach not only to *Tularosa* but to others of his books as well by observing that "he is a Code of the West, American Iliad man right down the line" (August 21, 1960).

Sonnichsen's account of the El Paso Salt War first appeared as a chapter in *Ten Texas Feuds* in 1957. The Salt War is discussed again in *Tularosa* and in *Pass of the North,* and in 1961 Sonnichsen's *The El Paso Salt War* was published by Texas Western Press. The typography is the work of the distinguished Carl Hertzog, and the book is impressively illustrated with drawings by Jose Cisneros.

The feud centered upon a salt bed which lies in the shadow of Guadalupe Peak and which, until the Civil War, had not been used. When various groups claimed the bed, the shooting started. It did not stop until the Texas Rangers were called in and the Mexicans made use of a firing squad. Sonnichsen concludes that "the Salt War, like all war, was wasteful and unnecessary, unless to prove to a pessimist that men can die bravely in a bad cause" (*El Paso Salt War,* p. 161).

Elmer Kelton praised the book for its "gripping style" (San Angelo *Standard Times,* August 6, 1961). Dale Walker of El Paso considered the publication by Carl Hertzog and Texas Western Press "a fitting tribute to the never-to-be-done-again grassroots work that had gone into this important chapter in El Paso history" (*C. L. Sonnichsen: Grassroots Historian,* p. 68).

Sonnichsen reasons that feuding occurred in Texas and the Southwest because from the "days of settlement, Texans have had more compulsion to fight than most people, more pistols and rifles to fight with and more opportunities and excuses for slaughtering each other" (*Ten Texas Feuds,* p. 5). Added to the fact that Texas existed a long time as a frontier state with both Indian and Mexican hostilities, the Southern Anglo settlers had a code of honor which insisted that every man should right his own wrongs "no matter what the teachings of Jesus or the law of the land said about it." Sonnichsen concludes: "Put the Code of the Frontier beside the Code of the Southerner, and you have the groundwork for conflict" (*Ten Texas Feuds,* p. 5).

Besides writing about people and feuds, Sonnichsen has applied himself to gathering other facts about his region. Either alone or in collaboration with others, he has written five books of history.

The major portion of *The Mescalero Apaches* is based upon official government reports, personal diaries, and newspaper articles. Interviews which cost the author "weary hours cornering old Indians who did not wish to talk to me or anybody else" ("Grassroots Historian," p. 382) gave substance and interest to the narrative. The book spans a period from the Spanish influence in 1540 to modern times, which have been marked by the building of tourist facilities on the reservation. The book, an outgrowth of unused material that was collected in the research for *Tularosa,* was given the Theta Sigma Phi Annual Writers Round-Up Award and *Desert Magazine's* award for the best book on Indians in 1958, and it was chosen by the Chicago Corral of the Westerners as one of the ten best books of 1958.

Of the many reviews of *The Mescalero Apaches,* few were unfavorable. Reviewing the book for the *Arizona Quarterly* in the summer issue of 1959, Peter Kunstadter found fault with Sonnichsen's opinion that the real trouble between Apaches and whites was due to a simple lack of understanding. The reviewer wanted Sonnichsen to look for more complicated reasons for Apache-white trouble. W. H. Hutchinson thought the book lacked "detailed anthropological data" and that Sonnichsen did not delve deeply enough into the Mescalero psyche, but the review added that none of the minor faults detracted "from the fundamental worth of the work . . ." (San Francisco *Chronicle,* December 28, 1958). Morris E. Opler lets his personal prejudice show through: "The author is not a historian but a professor of English in a college in the Southwest" (*American Anthropologist,* August 1959). Opler himself had done an anthropological study of Apaches, and "What right had an English professor to trespass in my dig?" he implies.

There was more praise than criticism. In England, Frederick Nolan pointed out that the book "has the great virtue, as do all those from this talented writer, of being extremely readable, and the bibliography indicates that much background research has gone into it" (*English Corral of the Westerners,* mimeographed sheet, December 1958). Wayne Gard commented: "Sonnichsen . . . makes the Mescalero Apaches human" (Dallas *Morning News,* December 21, 1958). The Houston *Chronicle* praised the book as history: "Sonnichsen is happily free of an academic style, administering his history as incidents that read like fiction" (Sister M. Agatha, Feature Magazine Section).

Sonnichsen is obviously sympathetic toward Indians, but he manages to keep his perspective. He knows that as a white man he may never be able to understand Indians completely or for that matter any culture not his own. He does not go to the lengths that Frank Waters went to in *Pumpkin Seed Point,* for Waters not only wants to understand Indians, but he also manages to become one, visions and all. Neither does Sonnichsen make his book a clinical analysis as an anthropologist might have done. Rather than going to either of those extremes, he takes the middle ground in the hope that each culture may yet learn enough from the other for its own enlightenment. He agrees with N. Scott Momaday, Dee Brown, and other such scholarly friends of the American Indian that the white man has committed terrible sins, but he hopes that the sackcloth-and-ashes syndrome may pass, that we may go from public soul-searching to more constructive attitudes. We are still in a period of examining all the facts. As Sonnichsen says, "We have to look at both extremes before we know where the middle ground is" (*Journal of Arizona History,* Spring 1974, p. 99).

Sonnichsen's interest in Apaches goes beyond grassroots history. He has a sizeable collection of literature about Apaches, and through it he is able to trace the White man's changing attitudes toward Apaches and perhaps all Indians. He insists that popular fiction has a powerful influence upon folk attitudes and public opinion. In "The Ambivalent Apache," an article published in *Western American Literature* (Spring 1974) and reprinted in *From Hopalong to Hud*, Sonnichsen uses both early and modern fiction to illustrate how writers have helped readers to view the Apache either as a bloodthirsty savage or a noble, brave, courteous child of the desert. He observes wryly that readers love Indians when Indians behave like whites.

The Mescaleros had received only a brief look until Sonnichsen detailed their history. Before Sonnichsen the history of El Paso had been relegated to an "oral anecdotal folklore approach" in such works as Owen P. White's *Out of the Desert* published in 1924 ((Dallas *Times Herald*, March 16, 1969). *Pass of the North: Four Centuries on the Rio Grande* is Sonnichsen's brightest achievement in history. It is a culmination of all he feels, knows, and has read about the El Paso he obviously loves. The Texas Institute of Letters gave Sonnichsen the Friends of the Dallas Library Prize for writing *Pass of the North,* which they judged to be the best book of fact in 1968.

El Paso is not just another border town. From the beginning of its history, it has been a strategic crossroads for Indians, Spaniards (who came for gold and to "make worried Christians out of satisfied savages"), and the vast conglomeration of people moving west. How these various cultures have met, mingled, and merged on the Rio Grande is what *Pass of the North* is all about.

A Dallas *Times Herald* reviewer commented that before the publication of *Pass of the North*, "Sonnichsen was perhaps the most unappreciated writer in the state. But then with the exception of Tom Lea none of the El Paso school of writers has been noted in Austin or Dallas. Readers and collectors of Texana are, of course, ahead of the critics and judges of the Institute [Texas Institute of Letters] in their awareness of Sonnichsen's previous efforts. *Pass of the North* is a noble book and will certainly receive the readership it deserves" (March 16, 1969).

Part of the pleasure in reading *Pass of the North* is the personal tone. El Paso's people are often referred to as "we" and its things as "ours." The tone conveys the feeling that El Paso belongs to Sonnichsen, as it surely does, and he lays rightful claim through all his other books which lead up to *Pass of the North*. The personal touch is one feature which makes the book different from similar studies of Southwestern cities like Paul Horgan's *Centuries of Santa Fe*. A gifted novelist, Horgan dramatizes and fictionalizes scenes from Santa Fe's past. Sonnichsen finds his drama in facts bolstered by the reminiscences of El Paso's old timers and by material from every other available source.

Seemingly all Sonnichsen had said in his previous books was prologue to *Pass of the North,* his finest achievement. All the kinds of people about whom Sonnichsen has written — outlaw, feuder, cattleman, Mexican, Indian, folk hero — have contributed to El Paso in its rise from village to city. Readers may find some of his other works more humorous or more easily read, but from a scholarly standpoint *Pass of the North* will become the authoritative work on the El Paso area.

Sonnichsen never hesitates to team up with fellow researchers to produce books or to get books into print. Sonnichsen wrote the introduction to and edited Morris Parker's *White Oaks*: *Life in a New Mexico Gold Camp, 1880-1900.* Parker was a mining engineer who was living in White Oaks in 1882. His reminiscences about the community were intended for his grandchildren, but Sonnichsen knew that more than Parker's family would be interested. The University of Arizona press brought the book out in 1971.

At the direction of the president of the State National Bank of El Paso and with assistance from M. G. McKinney, Sonnichsen began to write the history of that financial institution. With McKinney's help in research, the two completed *The State National Bank Since 1881*: *The Pioneer Bank of El Paso*, published by Texas Western Press in 1971. Sonnichsen livens up what might have been a dull book with a spirited introduction telling why patrons are so quiet and respectful when entering banks. He says, "Economists may tell us, 'It's only money,' but people who don't have much of it don't talk or think that way" (*State Bank*, p. ix). The most exciting chapter of the book deals with the Depression and with how the bank managed to keep its doors open during those hard times. One reviewer, David T. Dillon, thought the "descriptions of the people connected with the bank . . . are too saccharine to be wholly palatable. Nevertheless, the bank's history is impressive. It is the only bank which survived the bank runs of 1931" (San Antonio *Express News,* September 12, 1971, p. 3).

In 1974 the Arizona Historical Society published a handsome volume entitled *San Agustin*: *First Cathedral Church in Arizona* by George Chambers and C. L. Sonnichsen. The volume traces the history of the cathedral from 1859.

Sonnichsen's only book that does not fit snugly into one of the three categories just treated is his anthology, *The Southwest in Life and Literature*: *A Pageant in Seven Parts.* Sonnichsen's course in Southwestern Literature was the most popular course he taught and was certainly the one he enjoyed the most. It was enhanced by the use of his own anthology for a text. One critic observed that the book "brightened up a soggy field" (Dallas *Times Herald,* July 1, 1962). The *Saturday Review* commented, "Fortunately, now and then such a work as the present one appears. Its editor is respected by his colleagues as a historian and by the public as an eminently readable, good-humored, and factually reliable writer" (December 1, 1962).

The anthology is an appropriate book with which to end a survey of all Sonnichsen's major works, for it allows some observations about his personal philosophy of writing.

Sonnichsen admits that he has spent all his teaching life trying not to write like and think like a professor. He shows wittily his distrust for some in his profession. In an article entitled "The Folklore of Academe," Sonnichsen confesses, "I agree wholeheartedly that scholars, who are mostly professors, are a different breed of men." Paraphrasing the old racial slur, he admits, "I am not, I hasten to add, violently anti-professor. I am not ashamed to admit that some of my best friends are professors. But I don't think I would want my daughter to marry one." With tongue out of cheek, he values the hard working types who regard teaching as something of a sacred duty to be fulfilled pleasantly, employing skill and maintaining the interest of students. The new barefooted breed of scholar and professor gives Sonnichsen cause for concern. He generally characterizes a scholar as "a university professor who can qualify for a grant." Further he is "a specialist who publishes articles that nobody is curious about — and wants to teach his specialty no more than six hours a week to four graduate students for $20,000 for nine months, with allowance for a research assistant and for travel." Sonnichsen goes on: "Next to his passion for research and publication, his major ambition is to keep lesser scholars off the graduate faculty (he insists that they must publish ten articles in top scholarly journals, or one book and five articles before they are fit company for him). His favorite indoor sport is getting on programs of professional societies as critic or respondent and roughing up the rising young scholar who leaves his rear uncovered" (*Nova,* June 1973).

Sonnichsen closes his treatise on the scholar-professor with something of his own philosophic interpretation of his calling:

> If everybody lives by assumptions, then I must admit that I live by mine. I grew up in the grip of what is called the Puritan Ethic. I lived through the Depression when the world did not owe anybody a living or an education and it was a privilege to have a job. I had to perform all sorts of strange tasks to get through college, and I thought an education was priceless even though it was authoritarian, cognitive rather than affective, unconcerned about my emotional needs, based on lectures and textbooks, assignments and examinations, and oftentimes arduous, monotonous and painful to endure. As a result my mind is closed about certain things. I will always be immovably convinced that peace is better than war, that cleanliness is better than dirt, that hard work is better than idleness. I believe, and always will believe, that learning is better than ignorance — that learning is difficult and takes real effort, but is worth drudging for. I believe the wise should instruct the ignorant if they want to learn, and if the ignorant don't want to learn, they should go somewhere else. My folklore tells me that it is better to repair than to destroy — that only an idiot burns down the house because he doesn't like the bathroom. My experience tells me that nobody is being discriminated against if he has a chance to better himself, even though he has to start at the bottom.
>
> This makes me a conservative, a member of the establishment, probably a male chauvinist pig. Whatever

I am, I have to think I am right because these attitudes are my basic assumptions, my folklore. I have to believe that the people who are trying to take everything apart and put it back together another way will eventually return to sanity, that is, to my set of assumptions. I am obliged to hope that the scholar and the gentleman, in some form, will return to us and be respected again. But I am realist enough, or folklorist enough, to be aware that if and when he reappears, it will be with a different set of assumptions and I may not recognize him or like him. That, however, is the way things work out in this most peculiar, if the best, of all possible worlds. (*Nova*, June 1973)

Even the decor in Sonnichsen's office offers further proof that he has tried not to take his life as an exalted university professor too seriously. Other offices often display copies of illuminated manuscripts, modern and traditional paintings, and objects pertaining to the occupant's unique interests. On the wall of Sonnichsen's office hangs a cover from an old farm magazine. Pictured on the cover is a pink and white pig lying asleep, its head resting on top of another snoozing porker.

While Sonnichsen is quick to take a slap at prima donna professors, he also has no use for students who belittle their universities. In a commencement address at the University of Texas at El Paso on May 13, 1972, Sonnichsen compared a university education to a welding torch, saying that there must be a teacher to turn on the gas and strike a match to the process. He explained, "there is just one good way to know whether you have graduated from a good school with a degree that means something. Ask yourself if you had one teacher who changed your life and turned you on. If you had one — just one — this has been a good school for you" ("The Little

Blue Flame," *Nova,* October, 1972, pp. 11-17). Sonnichsen himself has often been the teacher and friend who has changed lives and has turned on many another hopeful student and writer. His generosity in editing manuscripts and in giving help to aspiring writers is legendary. Anyone who knows Leland Sonnichsen must agree with Jose Cisneros, noted El Paso artist and illustrator of Sonnichsen's books: "Very few people I know equal him in understanding, kindness and appreciation; not to mention his profound knowledge of history, his wisdom, his patience and his fluid conversation" (Letter, November 16, 1974).

Early in his career Sonnichsen realized that the El Paso area is a unique triptych displaying three distinct cultures against a geographic atmosphere of harshness, beauty, and isolation, and that realization has no doubt helped to make him the regional writer he is. The harsh landscape and the way it molds tough, thorny, colorful, robust people in its own image is never more important than the people themselves and their actions. The landscape is the foundation for his best literary achievements.

The landscape as the stern taskmaster reminded Sonnichsen of another time when men were moved to and fro according to nature's whims: that time when God's chosen wandered about in a similar desert, following their herds, disputing over water holes and birthrights. Biblical allusions make the analogy pointed. In *Tularosa,* Eugene Manlove Rhodes likens the cattlemen of the area to Isaac's herdsmen and the herdsmen of Gerar who quarreled with one another. Elsewhere, Sonnichsen describes a character as a "very young Samson among very tough Philistines" (*Tularosa,* p. 72). The importance of the coming of the railroad is characterized as the time when "Gabriel blew his horn over Tularosa." Important in the history of the Mescalero Apaches, Victorio came, like Ruth, to accept the fact that "their people were his people;

their gods were his gods" (*Mescalero Apaches*, p. 159). Sonnichsen notes humorously in *Ten Texas Feuds* that "Vengeance is mine! said the Lord. But in and out of Texas He has always had plenty of help" (p. 8). Not one of Sonnichsen's books fails to make use of Biblical expressions.

Sonnichsen's method and style make for easy reading. He usually takes a protagonist, places him on the stage of the Southwest, and moves his character from one scene to the next. We see the good and the bad of the man without the need of any labels. We find out who his friends were and were not, and who his kinfolks were. To illuminate his character, Sonnichsen uses reminiscences from people who know the person. To enlarge upon what has been established about the person, he digs up facts from newspapers, diaries, court records, and books. There is often a geography lesson in his books. He sometimes uses myth and legend, even if only to debunk them. Often a weather report is provided. Even dialogue appears, always used sparingly and always with a cautious reminder to the reader that someone could have said it but not necessarily as here related. While examples of all the elements of Sonnichsen's style appear in other books, they are most easily studied in *Colonel Greene and the Copper Skyrocket*.

The first chapter of *Colonel Greene* opens with a weather report of a great snowstorm which paralyzed New Mexico and West Texas in the winter of 1907. Sonnichsen next introduces Greene, warm and secluded in his private train car, and gives a physical description of him. The third chapter makes use of all kinds of printed records to indicate the strengths and weaknesses of the man, at the same time moving the main character across the landscape through a kind of plot which is the story of Greene's life in the West. There are hardships for the protagonist: difficulties in raising capital for his mining schemes, conflicts with Mexican authorities, his court trial for the alleged murder of Jim Burnett, and the death of his daughter. There are mini-geography lessons on the vast country through which Greene cut a swath.

Sonnichsen sometimes brings in certain legends only to indicate that they were unfounded. He points out, for instance, that Greene was usually portrayed "as a poor unlettered cowboy who had risen from rags to riches" (*Colonel Greene,* p. 3). Sonnichsen maintains, however, that Greene received a good education in New York state before coming to the West.

Even variations of the same story are recorded, always briefly, to show all sides of an issue, or simply to show how complicated matters can become. In telling about a shoot-out between Mexican strikers and Cananea mine men, the author reports, "Half a dozen variant versions tell how it happened. George did the shooting; George went down under the rush and Will did the shooting; somebody inside did the shooting" (p. 183). We are given even more variations on the theme, followed by the conclusion, "whoever was responsible, the damage was done. There were dead men of both races in the street, and worse trouble was coming" (p. 183).

Sonnichsen's narrative technique makes use of many of the tools of prose fiction as well as the trappings of drama. Some sections of his books could be acted out, as the following from *Colonel Greene*: " 'George, I tell you it's a big thing. It can make us both rich.' Greene gripped George Mitchell's arm as he spoke" (p. 47).

Throughout his career as a writer and teacher, Sonnichsen has always maintained a collection of Western fiction. *From Hopalong to Hud: Thoughts on Western Fiction* is a collection of essays in which Sonnichsen explores important, unimportant, good, bad, and all-the-shades-in-between fictional literature of the West. He believes that "in fiction — particularly Western fiction — we see our own faces" (*Hopalong to Hud,* p. 3). The book also reiterates one of Sonnichsen's theories about folklore, a proposition which says that what people choose to believe about the facts is a fact in itself.

Western novelists have probably done the most to establish certain Western stereotypes. These types are noticed particularly in the chapter subtitled "The Unheroic Cowboy in Western Fiction." Sonnichsen discusses the fictional-hero types beginning with Hopalong Cassidy. He explains, "With Hopalong as a model, the specifications for Hero status turn out to be quite simple. It can be demonstroted that the one and only trait which every fictional hero had to have was just plain guts" (*Hopalong to Hud,* p. 104). Sonnichsen finally traces the stages of development of the Western hero forward to Larry McMurtry's *Horseman, Pass By,* known to moviegoers as *Hud*. He points out that while a reviewer described the film as decadent and the hero as representing the dregs of Westernism, the publishing world insisted that the book painted a true picture of modern ranching life. "Either way," Sonnichsen continues, "*Hud* brings seventy years of doubt about the cowboy hero to final disillusion" (*Hopalong to Hud,* p. 126).

Other chapters detail the fictional treatment of such subjects as gunfighters, Apaches, Mexicans, sharecroppers, the town of Tombstone, and even "Sex on the Lone Prairee." All the essays in *From Hopalong to Hud* go straight to the heart of the matter, interpret logically, and show the truth or whatever reader's believe the truth to be. The reader is inclined to squirm when idols fall, but at the same time Sonnichsen points out that Western writers have told much of the truth. He sees as especially healthy the rash of modern parodies which restore some hope in the Western myth by poking fun at all the standard fictional characters and plots.

From Hopalong to Hud was favorably reviewed and received the Best Book Award for non-fiction from the editors of *Texas Books in Review* in 1978.

Sonnichsen is aware of how important the tools of fiction can be to a historian. In an article entitled "The Poetry of History," written for *American West* in August 1975, he points out that historians are often dull and become "a weariness unto student flesh" (p. 27). He thinks that training is partly to blame, for historians are taught to be objective, to refrain from using the first person ("thus making sure that the historian is left out of history"), and to abstain from jokes or ornamental words. The historian behaves as he should out of fear of criticism from other worthy historians. Sonnichsen quips: "Hell hath no fury like an authority on military history who catches a young scholar quartering the wrong military unit at Ft. Bowie in 1877" (p. 27). The irony of these restrictions upon the historian is that the reading public, in spite of the professional critics, honors writers like Irving Stone, Bruce Catton, and Bernard De Voto who "disregard the taboos and put the poetry back into history" (p. 27).

Sonnichsen explains his own methods of historical writing when he answers the question: How do you get the imagination in? "Can you document your poetry — your metaphors, your vivid language? A conscientious historian will not invent conversations — but if he knows what was said, he can put it into direct discourse. If he can find out what kind of day it was when the Indians attacked Custer . . . he can talk about the weather. If he has been there and knows what the country looks like, he can describe it. If he knows the chief character pretty well, he can explain his feelings and motives. If he has thought about causes and consequences, he can analyze them. If he wants to communicate feeling, there are openings which he can use without violating the decencies of scholarly writing" (p. 27).

Sonnichsen's light handling of words makes for humor which in turn makes for easy reading. In spite of material that could have become deadly dull because of the frequent killings, genealogies, and lengthy accumulations of facts, his narratives sparkle with a turn of phrase or funny incident. For example, in telling that Colonel Greene's wife heard him say "damn" only once in all their married life, Sonnichsen adds, "There are stories which indicate that he could do better in other environments . . ." (p. 88). When Jonny Ringo asked Frank Leslie if he ever shot anybody in the front, Frank replied, "I take them as they come" (*Billy King's Tombstone,* p. 31). Sonnichsen says of Ben Goodrich, early Tombstone lawyer, "He did not drink, he did not gamble, he never turned up in the red-light district. He didn't even go to church. In fact, he had no small vices" (*Billy King's Tombstone,* p. 162). The wife of Durkee, the freighter, was "the bell cow of the social herd" (*Billy King's Tombstone,* p. 162). We learn of an admirer of Etta Clark, the "madam" who lived in a palatial mansion: "An admirer of hers in the wholesale liquor business erected it for her in 1889 at a cost of $75,000. The deal also cost him his wife" (*State Bank,* p. 42). Sonnichsen says of El Paso in her roaring days, "El Paso was not exactly a wide-open town, but it was certainly standing ajar" (*State Bank,* p. 42). In describing Roy Bean's character and Beanville, the section of town to which Roy attached his name, he observes, "Anybody but Roy would have sacrificed a good deal to keep his name off the place" (*Roy Bean,* p. 54). Last, when Judge Bean handed down a decision: "The woman was to have the family burro . . . the man was to have fifteen minutes to get out of town" (*Roy Bean,* p. 170).

Those historians who deal only in facts give their readers instruction in dates, events, and names of people and places. The antitheses of such factual historians are folklorists whose major concern is not facts but is, rather, fascinating tales about people and people-ways, which often give different versions of the same events. Folklore is a branch of history which some pure historians scorn as unworthy of the name of his-

43

tory, although many intelligent readers prefer it to factual history. The synthesis of history and folklore is an approach to writing that appeals to a wide audience. Sonnichsen is the kind of historian who recognizes that people are as much a part of history as facts and that facts are more readable and satisfying when surrounded by scenery, by a feeling of historical time and place, and by fascinating tales. Sonnichsen agrees with Westerner Eugene Manlove Rhodes's philosophy that it takes at least three trees to make a row and it takes at least three facts to make a truth. The theory might stretch to include history — it takes three kinds to leave a well-rounded and accurate account. The frequent reprints and many favorable reviews of Sonnichsen's books attest to the fact that he is both a historian to be trusted and a folklorist to be enjoyed.

C. L. Sonnichsen has explored the lore and history of his region and writes about it with sympathy and understanding. In his hands the Southwest's outlaws, feuders, "madams," Indians, gamblers, cowmen, and hell-raisers turn out to be most interesting folks. Fortunately, we may expect more from him. Wherever his interest leads him, his readers have come to expect anything from his pen to be researched with care, written with skill, and embellished with wit. The vast Southwest becomes an even better place from having seen it through C. L. Sonnichsen's eyes.

Selected Bibliography

BOOKS BY C. L. SONNICHSEN

Sonnichsen, C. L. *Billy King's Tombstone.* Caldwell, Idaho: The Caxton Printers, Ltd., 1942.

———. *Roy Bean: Law West of the Pecos.* New York: MacMillan Company, 1943.

———. *Cowboys and Cattle Kings.* Norman: University of Oklahoma Press, 1950.

———. *I'll Die Before I'll Run.* New York: Harper and Brothers, 1951.

——— and William V. Morrison. *Alias Billy the Kid.* Albuquerque: University of New Mexico Press, 1955.

———. *Ten Texas Feuds.* Albuquerque: University of New Mexico Press, 1957.

———. *The Mescalero Apaches.* Norman: University of Oklahoma Press, 1958.

———. *The El Paso Salt War.* El Paso: Carl Hertzog and the Texas Western Press, 1961.

———. *The Southwest in Life and Literature: A Pageant in Seven Parts.* New York: Devin-Adair Company, 1962.

———. *Outlaw: Bill Mitchell alias Baldy Russell.* Denver: Sage Books, 1965.

———. *Pass of the North.* El Paso: Texas Western Press, 1968.

——— and Millard G. McKinney. *The State National Since 1881: The Pioneer Bank of El Paso.* El Paso: Texas Western Press, 1971.

———. *Colonel Greene and the Copper Skyrocket.* Tucson: The University of Arizona Press, 1974.

——— and George W. Chambers. *San Agustin, First Cathedral Church in Arizona.* Tucson: Arizona Historical Society, 1974.

———. *From Hopalong to Hud: Thoughts on Western Fiction.* College Station: Texas A & M University Press, 1978.

———. *The Grave of John Wesley Hardin.* College Station: Texas A & M University Press, 1979.

BOOKS EDITED BY C. L. SONNICHSEN

Parker, Morris B. *White Oaks: Life in a New Mexico Gold Camp.* Edited with an introduction by C. L. Sonnichsen. Tucson: University of Arizona Press, 1971.

ARTICLES BY C. L. SONNICHSEN

Sonnichsen, C. L. "Miss Sue Pickney and Her Private World." *Southwest Review,* 29 (Autumn, 1943), 80-82.

―――. "There Was Only One Roy Bean." *Around Here,* 2 (1944), 53, 76.

―――. "Tombstone: Outlaw Capital of the West." *Around Here,* 2 (1944), 66, 68, 82.

―――. [Crockett Clifton, pseud.]. "Robin Hood of the Cattle Country," *Around Here,* 2 (1944), 84.

――― and Frances Bramlette Farris. "The Domestication of Bigfoot Wallace". *Southwest Review,* 29 (Spring 1944), 429-436.

―――. "Bigfoot Wallace Brings the Mail," *Around Here,* 4 (1946), 72.

―――. [Samuel L. Clifton, pseud.]. "The White Sands Mystery." *Around Here* 4 (1946), 77, 85-86.

―――. "El Paso and the World's Championship." *Around Here,* 4 (1946), 87.

―――. [Samuel L. Clifton, pseud.]. "The Miller-Frazer Feud." *Around Here,* 5 (1947), 62.

―――. "Last of the Great Rangers: Captain John R. Hughes." *Around Here,* 5 (1947), 64.

―――. "The El Paso Train Robbery." *Around Here,* 5 (1947), 72.

―――. [Samuel L. Clifton, pseud.]. "Cold in them Hills." *Around Here,* 5 (1947), 80.

―――. "The Tragedy of the Gran Quivira." *Around Here,* 6 (1948), 54, 58.

―――. "New Deal for the Mescaleros." *Around Here,* 6 (1948), 56, 53.

―――. [Samuel L. Clifton, pseud.]. "Dog Canyon." *Around Here,* 6 (1948), 60, 64.

―――. [Samuel L. Clifton, pseud.]. "Black Jack Ketchum Died Game." *Around Here,* 6 (1948), 75, 82.

―――. [Samuel L. Clifton, pseud.]. "John Wesley Hardin – El Pasoan." *Around Here,* 7 (1949), 51, 76.

―――. "Victorio." *Around Here,* 7 (1949), 55, 67.

―――. "The Southwest's First Tourist." *Around Here,* 7 (1949), 59.

―――. [Samuel L. Clifton, pseud.]. "Pat Garrett Passes On." *Around Here,* 7 (1949), 54, 64.

―――. "The Apache Kid." *Around Here,* 10 (1952), 61-62.

―――. "Allison, Clay." *The Handbook of Texas,* I, ed. Walter Prescott Webb. Austin: The Texas State Historical Association, 1952. Also contributed other entries.

―――. "Major McMullen's Invasion of Mexico." *Password,* 2 (May 1957), 38-43.

―――. "A Feud for Miss Sue Pickney." *New Mexico Quarterly,* 27 (Autumn 1957), 171-184.

―――. "The Hermit of Dog Canyon." *New Mexico Magazine,* 36 (January 1958), 16-17, 44-45.

―――. "Pat Garrett's Last Ride." *True West,* 6 (November-December 1958), 4-6, 30-32.

――― and William V. Morrison. "They Killed Pancho Villa!" *Frontier Times,* 34 (Winter 1959-60), 6-10, 48-50.

―――. "The El Paso Train Robbery." *Password,* 6 (Spring 1961), 60-62.

―――. "Our Regional Literature." *Rodgers Library Notes,* 11 (April 1962), 1-2.

―――. "Richard Fenner Burges." *Password,* 8 (Spring 1963), 9-10.

―――. "Mitchell Escaped Everything, Even 'Stood Up' Death." *The Southwesterner,* 2 (April 1963), 7.

―――. "Justice After Dark." *True West,* 13 (January-February 1966), 18-20, 57-58.

―――. "The New Style Western." *The South Dakota Review,* 4 (Summer 1966), 22-28.

―――. "Tombstone in Fiction." *The Journal of Arizona History,* 9 (Summer 1968), 58-76.

―――. "Librarians Overlook Fiction: Fiction and History." *Kansas Library Bulletin,* 37 (Summer 1968), 14-15, 18.

―――. "The Wyatt Earp Syndrome." *The Roundup,* 16 (September 1968), 4, 6, 15. Appeared under the same title in *American West,* 7 (May 1970).

―――. "The Sharecropper Novel in the Southwest." *Agricultural History,* 43 (April 1969), 249-258.

―――. "The Grassroots Historian." *Southwestern Historical Quarterly,* 73 (January 1970), 381-392.

―――. "Footnote Fever: Confessions of a Research Addict." *Collector's Institute,* (November 1970), 15-23.

Carter, A. G. as told to C. L. Sonnichsen. "Neighborhood Talk About Pat Garrett." *Old West,* 7 (Fall 1970), 20-22, 62-64.

――― and M. G. McKinney. "El Paso—from War to Depression." *Southwestern Historical Quarterly,* 74 (January 1971), 357-384.

―――. "Col. W. C. Greene and the Cobre Grande Copper Company." *The Journal of Arizona History,* 12 (Summer 1971), 73-100.

―――. "Instant Millionaire: Colonel W. C. Greene in Fact and Fiction." *The American West*, 8 (November 1971), 4-9, 62-63.

―――. "Colonel William C. Greene and the Strike at Cananea, Sonora, 1906." *Arizona and the West*, 13 (Winter 1971), 343-68.

―――. "Treasure at Kern Place Pharmacy." *Texas Library Journal*, 48 (May 1972), 79-83.

―――. "The Little Blue Flame." *Nova*, 7 (October 1972), 11-13, 17.

―――. "The Folklore of Academe." *Nova*, 8 (June 1973).

―――. "Two Black Legends." *Southwestern American Literature*, 3 (1973), 5-21. Not actually issued until 1976.

―――. "Toward an Order of Minor Historians." *The American West*, 11 (March 1974), 48, 62-63.

―――. "UTEP, 'Harvard on the Border'." *Nova*, 9 (June 1974), 11-13, back cover.

―――. "The Poetry of History." *The American West*, 12 (August 1975), 26-27, 59-60.

―――. "The Ambivalent Apache." *Western American Literature*, 10 (August 1975), 99-114.

―――. "The Poor Wayfaring Scholar: Folklorist vs. Popular Culturist." *Journal of Popular Culture*, 10 (Summer 1976), 88-95.

―――. "Dracula in the Stacks." *Wilson Library Bulletin*, 51 (January 1977), 419-423.

―――. "The West that Wasn't." *The American West*, 14 (November-December 1977), 8-15.

―――. "The Grave of John Wesley Hardin." *Password*, 22 (Fall 1977), 91-107.

―――. "Sex on the Lone Prairee." *Western American Literature*, 13 (June 1978), 16-32.

ABOUT C. L. SONNICHSEN

Newman, Bud. "The Writings of C. L. Sonnichsen." In Dale Walker's *C. L. Sonnichsen: Grassroots Historian*.

Walker, Dale. *C. L. Sonnichsen, Grassroots Historian*. El Paso: Texas Western Press, 1972.

―――. "A Conversation with Doc Sonnichsen." *Nova*, 7 (February 1972), 1-6.